I Love My Grandmother Because . . .

Compiled by
Carolyn J. Booth
and Mindy B. Henderson

RUTLEDGE HILL PRESS®
Nashville, Tennessee
A Thomas Nelson Company

Copyright © 1998, 2001 by Carolyn J. Booth and
Mindy B. Henderson

All rights reserved. Written permission must be secured from the publisher to use or
reproduce any part of this book, except for brief quotations in critical reviews and
articles.

Published by Rutledge Hill Press®, a Thomas Nelson Company, P.O. Box 141000,
Nashville, Tennessee 37214.

Illustrations by Farrar Hood

ISBN: 1-55853-886-0

Printed in Colombia

1 2 3 4 5 6 7 8 9 — 05 04 03 02 01

Introduction

There will always be a special connection between a grandmother and her grandchildren. Our grandmothers give us unconditional love and wisdom learned throughout their lives. Sometimes they let us break rules and do things our parents don't usually allow! Whenever grandmothers and grandchildren spend time together, there will be a lot of love, a lot of fun, and a lot of precious memories to be treasured forever.

In this book, grandchildren of all ages share their special reasons for loving their grandmothers. Their words come from the heart. Some smile with joy when remembering happy times spent with their grandmothers, others' eyes fill with tears as they recall loving memories of a grandmother who is no longer with them.

Your own unique bond with your grandmother is very special. When you think about the reasons why you love your grandmother, write them down. Tell her how much you love her and why she is so precious to you. Give her a kiss and a big hug and spend some more time together making memories.

CAROLYN J. BOOTH

$\mathscr{B}$eing a grandmother ranks
right up there with becoming
a mother, only more fun and
less work!

*I Love My
Grandmother Because . . .*

She makes me

feel important.

We have family hugs with her
and Pop.

She has the most beautiful voice and
sings the sweetest songs. She lives far
away and sends me tapes of
her singing.

*H*ave you ever asked yourself why your parents' mothers are called your grandmothers? Of course you haven't, because everyone with a grandmother knows that *grand* is the perfect word.

*T*here is a first for everything—but there is nothing that compares to becoming a grandmother for the first time!

$\mathcal{G}$randchildren learn more from modeling than they do from advice.

$\mathcal{O}$ne day my daughter ran into my mother's house and yelled, "Let me see it!"

"What?" asked my mother.

"Your Grammy Award! You must have one!"

My mother beamed. She looked at me and then gave my daughter the biggest hug. "That's just for people in the music business, sweetie!"

"Well, you should have one, too," protested my daughter. "No one deserves a Grammy Award more than my grammy!"

*I Love My
Grandmother Because . . .*

She comes to all of my ball games.
Afterward, she takes me to the
concession stand and lets me buy
whatever I want.

She taught me
to knit.

She makes yummy
chocolate gravy!

*S*ometimes on cold nights, when I curl up under the red, white, and blue bicentennial afghan that my grandmother knitted me in 1976, I think it was not so long ago that she and I were watching the celebration. I see the fireworks in the sky. I remember the twinkle in her eyes. I remember the smile on her face, and I remember holding the small, wrinkled hand that knitted the warm afghan. I think of the stories about her that I will tell my children as we cuddle beneath the blanket, and I think of the stories that my children will tell their children as the afghan moves on through the years.

16

$\mathcal{T}$he simplest toy, one which
even the youngest child
can operate, is called
a grandparent.

—SAM LEVENSON

$\mathcal{I}$ love my grandmother
because when my dad gets
after me, she reminds him
that I am just like him.

*I Love My
Grandmother Because...*

We sit outside at night and talk about

anything I want to talk about.

She is my
favorite baby-sitter.

She is a
good listener.

My grandmother is a role model to me. Sometimes I will catch myself telling her about different feelings that I have or changes that I am going through. Just by the way she looks at me, I can see that she has been there before. She has been down these roads. She tells me that what I am today is made up of what I have experienced in the past. I see her, and I see her experiences. She is kind and loving. I long for my experiences to teach me to be the type of woman that she is.

$\mathscr{T}$he one thing we never give

enough of is love.

—HENRY MILLER

$\mathcal{I}$ love my grandmother because when I was three years old, she was telling me a very long story, and I asked her to please let her mouth go night-night! She didn't get mad, and she laughs about it to this day.

My grandmother is
the gem that gives sparkle
to my life.

I Love My
Grandmother Because . . .

I can make a mistake, and it is no big

deal to her. She just says,

"You'll do better next time."

She's my sweetie pie,
and I'm her sweetie pie.

She will read me my favorite story
over and over
and over again.

$\mathcal{C}$hildren have never been
very good at listening to
their elders, but they have
never failed to imitate them.

—JAMES BALDWIN

$\mathcal{S}$ome wise person once said
that hindsight is better than
foresight. That is what makes
being a grandmother
so wonderful! You can use
all your hindsight with
your grandchildren!

$\mathcal{I}$ love my grandmother because she tells me funny stories about my daddy when he was my age.

$\mathcal{W}$e're called Lolly and Pop

by our grandchildren.

Are we suckers for them?

You bet we are!

—LANELL PADGETT

*I Love My
Grandmother Because . . .*

She doesn't mind buying the cereal

that I see on television.

She puts magic cream
on my boo-boos and makes
them go away.

She is the best biscuit
maker in the world.

Children's children are a crown to the aged.

—PROVERBS 17:6

AS MY
Grandmother
USED TO SAY . . .

*I*f you see a book, a rocking chair, and a grandchild in the same room, don't pass up a chance to read aloud. Instill in your grandchild a love of reading. It's one of the greatest gifts that you can give.

—BARBARA BUSH

When I was younger, I used to hear all of the kids at school talking about their grandmothers. "Grandmother got me this." "Grandmother said that." I didn't understand why I didn't have a grandmother.

Finally, one day, I went home very sad.

"What's wrong?" my mother asked me.

"Everybody has a grandmother except me," I choked out to my mother, trying to hold back the tears.

"Why, Marsha," my mom said. "Everybody has a grandmother, but not everybody has a Go-Go. You have a Go-Go!"

I had always called my grandmother Go-Go. My older cousin had given her that name. I didn't know she was my grandmother! I just knew that whenever I visited her home, we would go all kinds of different places, like to the store, or the park, or the library. She lived in California, and before we even got our bags unpacked, she would excitedly begin to tell us about all the things we were going to do and the places she had planned to go. I was always excited to go to Go-Go's house because I knew that she would have someplace interesting and new to take me.

As I grew older and the kids talked about their grandmothers, instead of feeling left out and sad, I straightened my shoulders and thought to myself, "They may have a grandmother, but I have a Go-Go!" I was very proud.

—MARSHA GRIFFIN

*I Love My
Grandmother Because . . .*

When I think of her, I can smell her

spaghetti sauce. It is the best and

so is she!

She lets me rummage through
her jewelry box.

She says, "You are so pretty.
You look just like
your mother."

$\mathcal{A}$ good grandmother
keeps the vision of beauty
and instills this hope in her
children and grandchildren.

AS MY
Grandmother
USED TO SAY . . .

Remember to never talk badly about
your grandchildren's parents.

Remember to create memories that
will last forever.

Remember to listen with patience.

Remember to appreciate your
grandchildren's feelings.

Remember to share your spiritual
beliefs with your grandchildren.

I Love My
Grandmother Because . . .

She taught me about God.

I always sat by her at church.

She fixed a special room

at her house for me!

She tells me

I am perfect.

*A*ny great truth can—and eventually will—be expressed as a cliché—a cliché is a sure and certain way to dilute an idea. For instance, my grandmother used to say, "The black cat is always the last one off the fence." I have no idea what she meant, but at one time, it was undoubtedly true.

—Solomon Short

The secret of a happy life is
to skip having children
and go directly to
the grandchildren.

—FROM A MOMMA CARTOON BY MEL LAZARUS

I love my grandmother
because she puts my art all
over her refrigerator.

My son, age four, looked
at my mother the other day
and said, "Gram, are you
getting old?" "No!" she replied
quickly. "I'm not getting older.
I'm just getting happier." She
smiled and winked at him.

I Love My Grandmother Because . . .

When someone is mean to me, and
I tell her about it, she closes her fist
and says, "Do you want me to give
them five knuckles?"

She does funny faces to
make me laugh.

She comes to my
piano recitals.

$\mathscr{A}$ grandmother's stories
build strength and provide a
foothold for integrity, dignity, and
a sense of fearlessness. They give
direction, guidance, and
self-respect, define limitations, and
outline freedom.

—FROM *WALKING IN MOCCASINS*,
MUSEUM OF NORTHERN ARIZONA,
FLAGSTAFF, ARIZONA

*G*randmothers radiate
warmth and love.
They encourage, hug,
comfort, understand, and
teach us that we are loved.

When Barrett, Nola's daughter, was in the sixth grade, one of her friends laughingly told Nola, "Someday, when you are a grandmother, you will probably be called GranNola."

Years later, she did become a grandmother; and yes, her granddaughter, Hannah, calls her GranNola! It always makes for quite a laugh in the grocery store. People are so confused when Hannah calls out, "GranNola!" Does that child urgently want a granola bar? No, she just wants something sweeter! She wants her grandmother, GranNola.

—BARRETT DOZIER

$\mathscr{I}$ love my grandmother because she lets me pray for everyone I can think of before I go to bed.

I Love My
Grandmother Because . . .

She tells me about her and Paw Paw's

wedding and about my mommy and

daddy's wedding.

She lets me brush her hair
and play beauty shop.

She spoils
me rotten.

$\mathcal{F}$amilies will live on through
the stories we tell our children
and grandchildren.

*Y*oung Langston Hughes curled into his grandmother's lap as she wrapped him with a bullet-riddled shawl. He stroked the tattered shawl and listened as Grandmother Langston told how her first husband, Sheridan Leary, had gone to Harper's Ferry, Virginia, in 1859. She explained that Leary, a freeman, died at John Brown's side, fighting for the freedom of others, leaving the shawl behind as a symbol of his commitment to the cause.

Through Grandmother Langston's stories, Hughes learned to be courageous and to fight for his beliefs. She taught him to judge a man by his actions, not by the color of his skin, and that all people deserved to be free.

Langston Hughes died in 1967. His Kansas heritage and his grandmother's stories helped shape the words he shared with the world.

—Kansas State Historical Society

61

*I Love My
Grandmother Because . . .*

She is pretty and so sweet.
She loves me and all of my cousins
equally. She says we are like the
flowers in her garden. Each of us has
a unique beauty.

She has great stuff
in her attic.

She taught me to tie
my shoelaces.

My grandmother had a very special recipe for rice that she handed down to me and my sisters. When she passed away, we waited a very long time before we tried to make it. Now all of us have attempted on several occasions to duplicate the recipe. It just does not taste the same! Could it be that we don't have the secret ingredient that she must have added—her special love for us? We can't be sure, but it makes perfect sense to us.

—TERASA W. SAV

My grandma is in heaven, but when I do something special, my mom says, "I'm so proud of you, and Grandma would be, too."

*W*hat is unconditional love? My first remembrance of this kind of love was with my Mamie. She was my comforter, encourager, and my biggest fan. She was a retired schoolteacher and every night she would study with me. Once, we were conjugating Latin verbs. I was so tired of practicing that I threw a little fit and stormed from the room.

Later, feeling guilty about my behavior,

I walked back to her room to apologize
to her.

"David," she said, "You never need to
apologize to me for anything. I know you
would never do anything intentionally to
hurt me."

At the moment, I knew the meaning of
unconditional love. She had that for me, and I
for her. Isn't that a beautiful sign of a
grandmother?

*I Love My
Grandmother Because . . .*

She helped me make my doll's

clothes. That's how I learned to sew!

She is
very wise.

She taught me to
keep scrapbooks.

$\mathcal{O}$ne time I went to Grandma's house, and we made about thirty cookies in all different shapes. I took some home to my brothers, and now every time I go to Grandma's house we always make a lot of cookies.

—BRETT HENRY

The reason grandchildren and grandparents get along so well is that they have a common enemy—parents.

$\mathcal{I}$ love my grandmother
because when I married,
she created a special
cookbook with all of her best
recipes for me.

*T*here was an out-of-town grandmother who was dearly loved by her young grandson. Before he could even talk, he cried when she left to return home. She would always say to him, "I'll be back! I'll be back!" One day, as she was about to leave, he came to her with his arms outstretched, and she picked him up. He squeezed her neck, and his voice quivered through his tears: "Beback? Beback?" To this day she is called BeBack, and her grandson is confident that she will always be back.

—RULE BRAND

I Love My
Grandmother Because . . .

She always let me drink out of her fine

china cups when I was a child. I am

seventy years old, and I still drink my

coffee from a fine china cup.

She loves me
no matter what.

She taught me to fold napkins
and set the table.

Top Ten Names for Grandmothers

1. Grandmother
2. Grandma
3. Granny
4. Mawmaw
5. Nana
6. MiMi
7. Nannie
8. Me-Maw
9. Mama_____ (First or Last Name)
10. Grandmommy

My grandmothers are full of
    memories,
Smelling of soap and onions and
    wet clay,
With veins rolling roughly over
    quick hands.
They have many clean words to say.
My grandmothers were strong.

—MARGARET WALKER

$\mathcal{I}$can still picture my grandmother, pulling her rocking chair beside the table on which her old rotary phone sat. She would take her shoes off and put her feet on the air vent, which was right below the table. I can see her performing this ritual every day—calling to check on our grades, to find out how our day went, and to tell us that she loved us. She would have talked for hours if we had let her. Through her calls she touched our hearts.

$\mathcal{T}$imothy learned about God from his mother and grandmother when he was a small boy.

—2 TIMOTHY 1:5

*I Love My
Grandmother Because . . .*

She lets me lick the beaters when she

makes a cake.

She brings me a chocolate turkey
every Thanksgiving.

She made me a quilt with squares
of fabric that each told a story
about our family.

$\mathcal{P}$icture your grandchildren
as a rose garden. Some will
bloom beautifully. Others will
need to be thorned to grow.
Garden with the warmth of a
smile, with patience and love.
In your later years, your life
surely will be a bed of roses.

*Y*outh! Stay close to the young and a little rubs off.

—ALAN JAY LERNER

83

$\mathcal{M}$y grandmother is a great guide. She has taught me to look forward to new experiences and see how bright the future is.

*I Love My
Grandmother Because . . .*

She takes me on fun trips to places
like Disney World.

She likes to have tea
parties with me.

She has pictures of me
all over her house.

*B*ig Granny told her stories
of young love and yesterdays
with Granddaddy with a
twinkle in her eye and her
special little giggle. I feel love
just remembering her.

—DEBORAH ANDREWS

*I*n relating the blessings
that have come their way,
grandmothers teach
us gratitude.

$\mathcal{M}$y grandmother always wanted us to call her Dear Heart. When she held me for the first time, she told my mother that was the name she wanted me to call her because she said that I was the nearest and dearest thing to her heart. As the years passed, all of the children came to understand exactly what their grandmother felt—because they had the same love for her.

—MARTHA JOHNSON

$\mathcal{I}$ love my grandmother because she says that there is no one like me! I am a masterpiece! I am special.

I Love My Grandmother Because . . .

She doesn't give me clothes for presents—only really cool toys and money!

She doesn't make me take
naps if I don't want to.

She makes great grilled
cheese sandwiches.

$\mathcal{I}$ loved to go to my grandmother's house when I was little. We would play and laugh and have so much fun. She had a large cuckoo clock that fascinated me. My mother said that every time it would chime, I would run and watch the bird come out. My grandmother would stand beside me, and together we would announce with "cuckoos" whatever hour it was.

Because I loved the clock so much, whenever I would cry, my grandmother would do a funny face and say, "Cuckoo, Cuckoo," to cheer me up. That's why I call her Cuckoo Nana. She was so funny and always so happy! Now that old cuckoo clock stands in my house, and every time the clock chimes, I remember Cuckoo Nana and look forward to the day when I can hold my own grandchild in front of the clock and tell him or her about my grandmother, my Cuckoo Nana.

—JAMIE STOFKA

The real miracle of life
occurs when your child's child
is born.

My daughter's family lives up North; my husband and I live in Florida. When my daughter and her family come to visit in the winter, my daughter always says, "We're going to see sunshine!"

Therefore, my grandchildren call me Grandma Sunshine. I take it as a great compliment because when they visit me I want them to feel warmth, happiness, and everything else that the word "sunshine" connotes.

—MARY STAPLETON

$\mathcal{N}$obody can do for little children what grandparents do. Grandparents sort of sprinkle stardust over the lives of little children.

—ALEX HALEY

97

*I Love My
Grandmother Because . . .*

She encourages me to do my best and
try to make the honor roll.

She buys anything that I have
to sell for school.

She asks her friends to order
Girl Scout cookies from me.

$\mathscr{G}$randmothers don't have to be smart. They just have to know how to answer questions like, "Is God married?" and "Why do dogs chase cats?"

$\mathcal{E}$verybody should try to
have a grandmother,
especially if you don't have
a TV, because grandmothers
are the only adults who have
time to spare.

$\mathcal{T}$here are many special names for grandmothers that are really extensions of the mothers' names. They include Andmomma, Othermother, and Momma2. How special that children think of their grandmothers as the "other mommies" in their lives!

$\mathcal{I}$ love my grandmother
because she gives me what
I need when I need it . . . and
today I need ice cream.

*I Love My
Grandmother Because . . .*

She wrote me letters while I was at
camp, telling me how much she
missed me and some funny things my
grandpa had done while I was away.

She buys me Play-Doh and
finger-paints—the things my
mommy won't buy me!

She gave me my
mommy's doll.

$\mathcal{I}$ love my grandmother
because when she sees me,
just the look on her face says,
"I love you."

A little boy had bought his grandmother a book and wanted to inscribe the front with something really special. He racked his brain and suddenly remembered that his father had a book with an inscription that he was very proud of. So the little boy decided to copy it. You can imagine his grandmother's surprise when she opened her book, which was the Bible, and found it inscribed, "To Grandma, with the compliments of the author."

$\mathcal{G}$randmothers don't have to
do anything but be there.

*I Love My
Grandmother Because . . .*

When I spend the night at her house,
I am always awakened by the smell
of bacon and I know that a big
breakfast is waiting for me!

She gives
good hugs.

She taught me how to
make a garden.

*I*f your baby "is beautiful
and perfect, never cries or
fusses, sleeps on schedule and
burps on demand, is an angel
all the time" . . . you're
the grandma.

—TERESA BLOOMINGDALE

I love my grandmother because she lets me watch home videos of our family, and she laughs right along with me. She always makes me feel like I am the star of the movie.

Ten Famous People Influenced by their Grandmothers

1. **Maya Angelou**—African-American poet whose autobiographies include many stories told her by her grandmother.
2. **Hans Christian Anderson**—nineteenth-century Danish author whose grandmother told him folktales that he included in his stories.
3. **Alex Haley**—African-American author whose greatest success, *Roots,* was born of the genealogical history recited by his grandmother.
4. **Langston Hughes**—poet, writer, and preeminent interpreter of the African-American experience, who was raised by his grandmother.
5. **Sir Walter Scott**—often considered the inventer of the historical novel, his grandmother entertained him as a child with stories of their ancestral Scottish border country.

114

6. **Eleanor Roosevelt**—wife of President Franklin D. Roosevelt and activist for the poor, youth, and minorities who was raised by her grandmother.
7. **James Madison**—fourth president of the United States, who was tutored until age eleven by his grandmother, Frances Madison.
8. **Sir Isaac Newton**—English scientist, astronomer, and mathematician, described as "one of the greatest names in the history of human thought," who was raised by his grandmother from age three to eleven.
9. **Alexander I**—Czar of Russia (1801–25), who was taken at birth by his grandmother to supervise his preparation to assume the throne.
10. **Hiawatha**—fictional Ojibwa hero of a poem by Henry Wadsworth Longfellow, who was raised by Nokomis, his wrinkled and wise grandmother, "daughter of the Moon."

*I Love My
Grandmother Because . . .*

She helps me with my homework.

She knows all about math.

She puts my juice in a coffee
mug so I can feel big!

She tells me fascinating stories in
which the heroine is a girl my
age with my name.

Foreign Grandmother Names

Dutch: *Grootmoeder*
French: *Grand-mére*
German: *Oma, Grossmutter*
Hawaiian: *Kupuna wahine*
Hungarian: *Nagyanya*
Italian: *Nonna*
Japanese: *Solo, Obachan*
Norwegian: *Farmor, Mormor*
Polish: *Babka*
Portuguese: *Avozinha*
Spanish: *Abuela*
Yiddish: *Bubbie*

$\mathcal{Y}$ou don't have to look like

a granny to be one.

*T*he oldest of five children, I was first to marry and first to present my parents with a grandchild. We lived close to my parents and we visited often. We all called my mother "Mama." I had a little brother just eight years old when my baby, Virginia, was born.

Whenever we would visit, Virginia would hear me, my three sisters, and her eight-year-old uncle call my mother Mama. One day, in her wide-eyed innocence, she went up to my mother and asked, "Are you my mama, too?"

"Yes, I am!" she said. And from that moment on, she has been Mama Too to all ten of her grandchildren.

—Camille Lowe

You don't think it's possible
to love your grandchildren any
more than you do today . . .
but then tomorrow comes.

*I Love My
Grandmother Because . . .*

Everybody that comes to her house at
Halloween gets the same treat except
for me—I get a special
grandkid's treat!

If I need her,
all I have to do is call.

She e-mails me cool
websites and jokes.

My Grandma Always Says . . .

"If you eat too much candy, your teeth will
    fall out."

"Pretty is as pretty does."

"Chew with your mouth closed."

"You look just like your mother (father)
    when you do that!"

"Carrots make your eyes strong."

"You are Grandma's precious angel!"

"If your momma and daddy say no, you
    just call me!"
"Tell Grandma all about it."
"Come let me kiss it."
"You know no matter what, I love you!"
"What's the magic word?"
"Be sure to say your prayers."

While vacationing in Hawaii, I found myself at the pool one day, surrounded by children playing and swimming. I kept hearing them say, "Honey, watch this!" and "Look, Honey!" At some point, I looked over to see who this Honey was that these children obviously adored. There, sitting by the pool, was their sweet, white-haired grandmother, laughing with them and clapping for their every talent!

Now that I am a grandmother, I'm teaching my grandbaby to call me Honey. I can't wait until she gets old enough to show off for me!

—EMBRY SAVAGE

We all know grandparents
whose values transcend
passing fads and pleasures
and who possess the wisdom
of distilled pain and joy.

—JIMMY CARTER

*I Love My
Grandmother Because . . .*

If my mommy is working, she comes
and picks me up at school when I am
sick and brings me home with her and
takes care of me.

She has a good
shoulder to cry on.

She lets me push the buggy
in the grocery store.

A grandmother recently met her friend for lunch. She started to tell her about her granddaughter and was cut short with this remark, "Before you start, I demand equal time, and I have ten grandchildren!"

*I*f I'd known grandchildren
were going to be so much fun,
I'd have had them first.

$\mathscr{A}$ priceless memory—
when your twelve-year-old
grandson hugs you after his
ball game even though his
buddies are standing around.
Then you know
you are special.

—CAROLYN BOOTH

I Love My Grandmother Because . . .

She comes to my school

to eat lunch with me.

She gives me
bubble baths.

She makes cupcakes for
my class at school.

Great Ways to Help Your Grandchildren Remember You

1. Have a special story that you read to them.

2. Make a tape recording of special memories of your family history, of their parents' experiences, or of your feelings the first time that you held them.

3. Find out what their favorite food is and always have that available to them whenever they are at your house.

4. Sing a special song to them each time they are around.

5. Videotape yourself reading a book, telling funny stories, or even talking about your family history.

6. Develop a special code—whether it be a look, a pat, or a phrase that is special between only you and them.

7. Start a tradition with them that is special only to them. For instance, send them a special flower on their birthday every year.

$\mathcal{B}$ecoming a grandmother
is like having dessert.
The best is saved for last.

$\mathscr{I}$ love my grandmother because she has shown me how to pause, enjoy the moment, and see the beauty that surrounds me.

I Love My
Grandmother Because . . .

She makes every holiday and birthday

a very special occasion.

She taught me to
follow my heart.

My secrets are
safe with her.

Grandma's Hands

I reached out for her hand to hold
To guide me through the mall.
My grandma took good care of me
When I was very small.

And as I grew she saw in me
The things I didn't know.
She always said, "You're good inside.
Your heart will grow and grow . . ."

I reached out for the hand to hold
That made my clothes for me,
That cooked my favorite cookies,
And bandaged up my knee.

That wiped tears from my eyes . . .
Picked flowers for my hair . . .
And intertwined each time
That we would say a prayer.

I reached out for her hand to hold
Before I went down the aisle
To marry the man I loved with
The approval of her smile.

And as grandma got older
I'd consult her for advice.
She'd patiently sit and talk with me,
Oh . . . our talks were so, so nice.

Now the years have come and gone,
Though it's hard to understand.
Now when I am with her . . .
She reaches for my hand.

I gladly take good care of her,
I hold her in my heart . . .
And as I hold her hand I know
We'll never be apart.